SPLITTING SELVES

(A Comparative Study of Indo-Eastern and Indo-Western Diaspora Literature)

Dr. Vipul Solanki

© All the rights are reserved with Dr. Vipul Solanki. No part of this book can be reprinted or professionally used without the prior – written permission of him.

Published by:
CreateSpace Publications

ISBN: 978-93-87771-05-5

1st Edition 2017

December 2017

Price: 8$

Dedicated to

My mother, Smt. Jyotiben R. Solanki

whose sacrifices have made this journey possible.

Index

Chapter – I	Introduction	01-30
Chapter - II	*The Namesake* and *Evening is the Whole Day* in the Light of Each Other: A Comparative Study	31-67
Chapter - III	Splitting Selves	68-73
	Bibliography:	74-78

Acknowledgement

This work has been an enlightening journey of learning. I take an opportunity to express my sincere gratitude to those who have encouraged and helped me to accomplish this work. Such a good work would not have been possible without the support of family, relatives, friends, and well-wishers.

I express my profound sense of gratitude to Dr. Jaydipshinh K. Dodiya, Professor, Department of English and Comparative Literary Studies, Rajkot as well as other teachers at the Department. I am extremely thankful to them for there insightful guidance and kind encouragement that made this work a pleasant journey.

I would rather prefer to show my love than to be thankful to my parents and all other family members for their kind support. I also thank my wife Hetal for her continuous love and support in this work.

I am indeed indebted to the publisher of this book for acknowledging the worth of the work and encouraging me to take it further for publication. Thank you very much.

My sincerest regards to all!!

Dr. Vipul Solanki

About the Book:

This work explores a kind of new in itself comparative study. So far, sufficient work has been done in Indian Diaspora literature. Specifically, a lot of work has been done in the area of Indian-Western Diaspora literature. Many writers have articulated the expatriate experiences of the Indians who have migrated to the Western countries. But, not much has been said about the expatriate experiences of those Indians who migrated to other Asian countries. Since centuries, particularly during the colonial period, many Indians have migrated to the countries which are on the Eastern side from India popularly known as Southeast Asian countries. There has been a lot of cultural exchange but least as been noted about it. There are only a few writers who have articulated these expatriate experiences.

The book explores the way expatriate experiences have been articulated of those who have migrated to the West from India, particularly to America and those who have migrated to East from India, particularly to Malaysia. These two are the completely distinct expatriate traditions. The Indian Western Diaspora literature chiefly deals with the themes like cultural dislocation while the Indian Eastern Diaspora literature deals with an altogether different set of themes. This book essentially explores these two distinct Diaspora literary traditions through a comparative study of Jhumpa Lahiri's *The Namesake* and Preeta Samarasan's *The Evening is the Whole Day*.

Chapter – I

Introduction

I

In these days, novel has gained its own unique stand among all other literary genres. Novel is the most popular literary form read widely across the world. Novel, in actual, touches the various issues of life and presents them with a naval approach, zeal, and vision as done in the debut novels *The Namesake* and *Evening is the Whole Day* by Jhumpa Lahiri and Preeta samarasan respectively.

In common terms, Novel is an elaborated story written in prose. M. H. Abrams, in *A Glossary of Literary Terms*, comments on application of the terms and in a way defines the form Novel as

> "…the term 'novel' is now applied to a great variety of writings that have in common only the attribute of being extended works of fiction written in prose."[1]

It is more elaborated than short story and longer than a novelette. Its popularity highly depends on its magnitude. An author's desire to express himself prompts him to take up writing and readers' interest in people and their doings make them read; this concept along with the level-headedness of the form made Novel the most popular form among readers. The term for the Novel in most European languages is '*roman*', derived from '*romance*'. This suggests that the form has its root elsewhere in the medieval literature of ancient European languages. English borrowed the word 'Novel' from Italian '*Novella*' meaning 'a little new thing'. In earlier days, Novels were used to be of moderate length and mostly loose in plots. But with flow of time, and with number of influences the Novel has now become fully grown up form of literature.

II

Keeping in mind the relevance and important of novel form among other literary genres, I propose to study two different novels comparatively. One is *The Namesake* and second is *Evening is the Whole day*.

This research work, a comparative study of *The Namesake* by Jhumpa Lahri and *Evening is the Whole Day* by Preeta Samarasan primarily observes novel and its various features in different regions like the further Eastern Asian country Malaysia and the Western country America. The research tries to analyze the form, plot construction, language, various narrative techniques, the different postmodern experiments done with the form, themes and presentation of novels in present time, characters in novel, novel with reference to Indian English Literature, novel with reference to expatriate writing and influences of various cultures and time on novel and its themes etc. with reference to *The Namesake* and *Evening is the Whole Day*.

Through the comparative study of the novels *The Namesake* and *Evening is the Whole Day*, this research work attempts to evaluate the various issues from different standpoints. This work is not only a comparative study of two different novels mentioned above but of many other things of literary world. This research work studies two different diasporic literary traditions like Indo-US diasporic writings and Indo-Malay diasporic writings. It also studies different cultures comparatively like the American culture, Malay culture, Indian culture and the culture that has emerged by the migration of Indians to America and Malaysia. The work looks at the cultural confluences come to an existence by the movement of globalization in postmodern era. This work also observes two post modernists, post-colonial, diaspora female writers: Jhumpa Lahiri and Preeta Samarasan. This work juxtaposes two novels and tries to interpret various issues like culture, history, society, language, and how the people get affected by it in East and West.

III

Before the various prime issues are focused, it would be better to talk what comparative study of literature is. The study of comparative literature is as old as single literature. Comparative Literature does not confine itself to any particular language or country nor does it create relationships with any single literature. It moves irrespective of any particular discipline. This will become clear in this definition by David Damrosch,

> "Comparative Literature is the study of literature beyond the confines of one particular country and

> the study of the relationships between literatures on the one hand and other areas of knowledge and belief such as the arts(e.g. painting, sculpture, architecture, music) philosophy, history, the social sciences(e.g. politics, economics, sociology), the sciences, religions etc. on the other hand. In brief it is the comparison of literature with other spheres of human expressions."[2]

It is clear that comparative literature is not confined to the literature of one country. To compare one author with another, one literature with another, the literature of one period with that of another, one literary genre with the other arts is the traditional activity of the literary scholars and the critics. With the emergence of national literature the scope of such comparison cuts across linguistic frontiers as well as national boundaries.

In other words Comparative literature is an interdisciplinary field whose practitioners study literature across national borders, across time periods, across languages, across genres, across boundaries between literature and the other arts (music, painting, dance, film, etc.), across disciplines (literature and psychology, philosophy, science, history, architecture, sociology, politics, etc.). Defined most broadly, comparative literature is the study of "literature without borders."[3] Scholarship in Comparative Literature include, for example, studying literacy and social status, studying medieval epic and romance, studying the links of literature to folklore and mythology, studying colonial and postcolonial writings in different parts of the world, asking fundamental questions about definitions of literature itself. What scholars in Comparative Literature share is a desire to study literature beyond national boundaries and an interest in languages so that they can read foreign texts in their original form. Many comparatists also share the desire to integrate literary experience with other cultural phenomena such as historical change, philosophical concepts, and social movements.

Hence, the following traits of Comparative Literature can be derived. It is the study of literature not in isolation, but in comparison. It can be a comparison of two or more similar or even dissimilar forms or trends within a span of literature of the same language, for example a comparative study of the psychological conflict of Hamlet and Don Quixote. Secondly, it can be a comparison of similar and dissimilar forms and trends in literature of two or more languages, for example, a comparative study of Romantic poets with reference to Keats in English and Ramesh Parekh in Gujarati or the *Vicar of the Wakefield* in English and Raja Shekhara's *Charitra* in Telugu. It is obvious that the trends of one literature are important to establish a comparison with another literature in more than two languages.

The intention of most of the scholars of Comparative Literature is to increase the understanding of other cultures, not to assert superiority over them. The same effort is done in this research work also. By comparing *The Namesake* and *Evening is the Whole* Day, from altogether geographically two different opposite directions, East and West, this research tries to bring out the qualities of these different cultures and their literary traditions.

IV

This research work is a comparative study of American culture and Malay culture, the heterogeneous societies made up by the migration of Indians to America and Malaysia, the generation gap between the first migrated generation and their own children born and brought up in immigrated nation, the confluences of languages that is created by the heterogeneous societies, the different diasporic traditions and many more issues are observed by juxtaposing the two novels.

As it is said earlier East-West encounter and cross-cultural encounter are the recurring themes of Indo-English fiction writing among the various other themes. This theme of cross cultural encounters takes an eminent place primarily after 1980. With the development of technology and the concept of Globalization the world becomes a small place. More and more people started to migrate in other countries from India. The place where they migrate forms a new picture of mélange of cultures, a confluence of more than one culture. In that sense it becomes the cross-cultural encounter, and the writer who gives voice to this issues by migrating themselves in other countries are called Diaspora writers. The Diaspora writers belong to two nations.

Increasingly the terms 'expatriate' and 'Diaspora' are gaining popularity. The word Diaspora is literally a scattering carrying within it the ambiguous status of being both an ambassador and a refugee. The requirements of two roles are different. While one requires the projection of one's culture and the ability to enhance its understanding, the other seeks refuge and protection and reacts more positively to the host culture. Further categories emerge through the use of such words as immigrants, exile, forced exile, alienation, and refugee. In Indian context perhaps all meaning are true with migratory movements having been governed by different reasons at different times of history, and different reasons even contemporaneously. Economic reasons governed by the movement of indentured labor and of the trading communities, they have also pursuit of a higher standard of living. Opportunities for work, research and freedom have motivated migration. Again migration from a colonial state to a free country calls for an entirely different set of assumptions than migration from one free nation to another. In the same way to migrate from an Eastern country to Western country also demands different approaches.

V

Indian English literature is an answer to the subaltern where the Indian writers in English Indianized the language of their colonizers. The arrival of the British in India led to popularization of Western education. Under the British rule, people were studying in English and it became a means of communication for the Indians with the rest of the world. To make their voice and creativity reach out to the world they took the aid of English language. Litterateurs like Rabindranath Tagore translated their works into English. Apart from him, writers like Michael Madhusudan Dutt, Toru Dutt, Sarojini Naidu, Mulk Raj Anand, R. K. Narayan, and several others chose English as the medium. With changing times and genres Indian English literature underwent several changes in its narratives and forms. Literary genres like post-colonialism, modernism, post-modernism affected Indian English literature too.

Fiction has come to be the most popular literary medium of expression today for Indo-Anglian writers. It is a genre that has gained a firm hold beneath its ground with the passage of time. Indian writers writing in English have evaluated norms and themes which are universal in their appeal, though rooted in the Indian social, political and historical climate of the country.

Drama, epic and lyric have been popular in India for several centuries. Even we have some of the greatest tradition of narratives yet the *novel*, as a literary form, was new to India. It is only during the last one hundred and twenty-five years that the novel has planted its roots in India. With the introduction of English in India, there was a spurt of translations. A number of English works were translated into some Indian languages. Gradually Indians also started writing novels in English. Bankim Chandra Chatterjee published his novel, *Rajmohan's Wife* in English in 1964. His other novels like *Durgesh Nandini*, *Kapala Kundala*, *Vishavriksha* and *Anadmath* appeared first in Bengali and later in English. Chatterjee translated the novels himself from Bengali to English. Some notable novels published in the same period, that is from 1864 to 1910, include; Rajlakshmi Devi's *Bianca* or *The Young Spanish Maiden* (1878); Kalicharan Lahiri's *Roshianara* (1891), and Ramesh Chander Dutt's *The Lake of Palms* (1902), and *The Block Fire of Agra* (1909). It was the publication of Rabindranath Tagore's *Home and the world* (1919), *The Wreck* (1921), and *Gora* (1923), which appeared first in Bengalis and later in English.

Though fiction writing began in the 19th century in India, the significant era began with Mulk Raj Anand (b. 1905), R. K. Narayana (b. 1906) and Raja Rao (b. 1908). These writers, under the impact of India's freedom struggle and nationalism, strived to portray not only their national concerns but also the social conditions of their times.

Mulk Raj Anand's major works, *Coolie* (1936) and *Untouchable* (1935) are a plea for the downtrodden – who face economic hardship and humiliation in a rigid social structure. He wrote other important novels like *Two Leaves and a Bud* (1937), *The Village* (1939), and *Across the Black Water* (1940) among others. He wrote under the impact of Gandhism, sought to awaken a new consciousness in the average thinking individual.

R. K. Narayan depicts the social realism through his works. His first novel *Swami and Friends* (1940) created a new sensibility, which was followed by the novels like *The Bachelor of Arts* (1936), *The Dark Room* (1938), *The English Teacher* (1945), *The Financial Expert* (1952), *Waiting for Mahatma* (1955) and *Guide* (1958). In his works, there is a flight, an uprooting, a disturbance of orders – followed by a return, a renewal, a restoration of normalcy.

Raja Rao, also a child of Gandhian age, reveals in his works sensitive awareness of the forces, led by Gandhian Revolution as also of the thwarting or steadying pools of the past tradition. His three novels are *Kanthapura* (1938), *The Boyfriend, The Serpent and the Rope* (1960), *The Cat and Shakespeare* (1965). Raja Rao was the first Indian writer to explore man's quest for self. His *Serpent and the Rope* revolves around this spiritual theme.

Thus, the emergence of 'the big three' – Mulk Raj Anand, R. K. Narayan and Raja Rao – on the literary firmament brought new hopes to the creative activity in the form of fiction. William Walsh states that,

> "It was in 1930s that the Indians began what has now turned out to be their very substantial contribution to the novel in English and one peculiarly suited to their talents"[4]

Falling in the line with the same pattern and theme Bhabani Bhattacharya's (b. 1906) *So Many Hungers* (1947), followed by *Music for Mohini* (1952), *He Who Rides a Tiger* (1954), *A Goddess Named Gold* (1960) and *Shadow form Ladakh* (1966) – form an impressive achievement of his writing. The personal and national issues form a fine blend to give to these novels its universal appeal. The contemporary of Bhattacharya is Manohar Malgaonkar. His collection of novels reveals a sound historical sense. He has published four novels in the course of five years: *Distant Drum* (1960), *Combat of Shadows* (1962), *The Princess* (1963) And *A Blend in the Ganges* (1964).

Kamala Markandaya's (b. 1924) novels, *Nectar in the Sieve* (1954) and *A Handful of Rice* (1966), portrays the harsh economical reality in the rural India. Her notable works are *Some Inner Furry* (1957), *A Silence of Desire* (1961), *Possession* (1963) and *The Coffer Dams* (1969).

Her marks as a novelist of Indian English fiction is the sufficient and suggestive of her prose.

Arun Joshi, with his novels *The Foreign* (1968) and *Strange Case of Billy Biswas* (1971), gives glimpses of man's quest for identity and his ability to retain his calm, poise and dignity in spite of heavy odds. His other significant works are *The Apprentice* (1974) and *The Last Labyrinth* (1981).

Ruth Prawer Jhabwala (b. 1927) has published six novels on the span of a decade: *To Whom he Will* (1955), *The Nature of Passion* (1956), *Esmond in India* (1958), *The Householder* (1960), *Get Ready for Battle* (1962) and *A Backward Place*. Her novels revolve around the theme of marriage and alienation. Atiya Singh remarks: "Jhabvala takes an amused look at arranged marriages in India with her Jane Austenian tongue in the cheek style."[5]

Nayantara Sahgal's (b. 1927) fiction takes a stand against vital relationship like marriage going sterile. All her novels, *A Time to be Happy* (1958), *This Time of Morning* (1968), *Storm in Chandigarh* (1069), *A Situation in New Delhi* (2008) portrayed a theme of marriage, with major political events in background. Her other works that voice women's plight are *A Day in Shadow* (1971) *Plans for Departure* (1985), *Mistaken Identity* (2007), *Lesser Breeds* (2003), and *Rich Like Us* (1983). Atiya Singh notes, "However, what makes them stand apart, is her bold proclamation of freedom for women, especially in their personal lives"[6]

Anita Desai's (b. 1937) novels *Cry the Peacock* (1963), *Voices in the City* (1965), *Bye Bye Blackbird* (1971) explore the woman's inner consciousness. Her later works are *Where shall we Go this Summer?* (1982), *Clear Light of the Day* (1980), *Village by the Sea* (1989), *Bumgartner's Bombay* (2000), *Fasting Feasting* (2000), *Fire on the Mountain* (2001), *Journey by Ithaca* (1996) and *In Custody*. Her novels take a closer look at concept of alienation and man's brooding sense of meaningless existence in the modern world.

Though contemporaries, Anita Desai and Nayantara Sahgal are virtual contrast in the portrayal of female characters and their attitudes to marriage. While Anita Desai's female characters desperately struggles to make their marriage a success, howsoever unfulfilling they may be, Sahgal's heroines opt out of it.

Political history of India also finds a new form in Indo-Anglian literature. The partition of India in 1947 and its violent aftermath was a traumatic experience for many. The deep wounds of partition reflected in many works. Khushwant Singh's *Train to Pakistan* (1956) highlights the theme of partition and its trauma. The novel spells new kind of human values and noble sacrifices are underlying themes of the novel. Khushwant Singh continues the trend with his new novel *Burial at Sea* (2004). The novel is based on happenings behind the sea during the Nehru years.

The partition trauma lingers in the consciousness of many writers. Of the novelist whose works appeared first in 70s, the most outstanding is Chaman Nahal. As for the novels, five have made their bow in quick succession: *My True Faces* (1973), *Azadi* (1975), *Into Another Dawn* (1977), *The English Queens* (1979) and *The Crown and the Loincloth* (1981). Chaman Nahal has used history as a metaphor in his writings.

V. S. Naipaul is the most celebrated and widely recognized among readers as well as critics. Being an Indian by ancestry, and living a suitcase life between three countries, Naipaul is the foremost among expatriate writers. His famous works are *The Mystic Masseur*, *The Suffrage of Elvira*, *Miguel Street*, *A House for Mr. Biswas*, *Mr. Stone and the Knights Companion*, *The Mimic Men*, *A Flag on the Island*, *Guerrillas*, *In a Free State*, *A Bend in the River*, *The Enigma of Arrival*, *A Way in the World* and *Half a Life*.

One of the sensational literary events of 80s was the publication of the Indian born Salman Rushdie's oversized novel, *Midnight's Children*, which has won the Booker Prize as well as James Tait Black Memorial Prize. The novel focuses on the political history of India during independence. Rushdie's other works include: *Grimus*, *Satanic Verses*, *East West*, *The Ground Beneath her Feet*, *The Moor's Last Sigh*, *Fury Shame*, etcetera. In 80s, there has been a fresh spurt of writing by a whole lot of new writers who are making Indo-Anglian fiction richer.

Another writer without roots, Rohinton Mistry, wrote not-so-prolific-yet-potential set prose. His novels are: *A Fine Balance*, *Such a Long Journey*.

The 90s witnessed a great surge of novel writing with the arrival of Amitav Ghos, Vikram Seth, Upmanyu Chatterjee, P. Rangarao and Nina Sibal. From social realism to pre and post partition trauma, to man's quest for self, it has been a long march for Indo-Anglian fiction.

Vikram Sheth's *The Golden Gate* (1986), a humorous satire on the fallibilities of west, marks a change in the trend of depending themes related to one's nationality or native soil. *A Suitable Boy* is Vikram Seith's another bulky book which has changed the art of narration.

Amitav Ghosh's *The Circle of Reason* (1986) is another step in portraying social realism garbed in fantasy. His other novels are *The Culcutta Chromosome*, *In an Antique Land*, *Dancing in Cambodia*, *At Large in Burma*, *Countdown* and *The Glass Palace*. Antony Burgess has called Ghosh a 'brain' and said that, "American writers could technically learn a lot from him."[7]

Upmanyu Chatterjee's *English, August: An Indian Story* (1988) deals with the theme of the pettiness and absurdities of the bureaucratic system and the alienation of the urban India. His later works are *The Last Burden* and *The Memories of the Welfare State*, which in turn is a sequel to *English, August*.

Rangarao's *Fowl–filcher* has attracted considering amount of literary attention in India and abroad. The bunch of Indian English writers is varied in style, content and purpose. But what distinguishes them from the earlier Indo-Anglian authors is their confidence and unselfconscious approach to the writing. One of the most well-known political works in the genre is Shashi Tharoor's *The Great Indian Novel* (1988), which parodies the epic structure of Mahabharata to analyze India under Indira Gandhi.

With Arundhati Roy's *The God of the Small Things* (1997) the Indian fiction reaches a new pinnacle. With Booker Prize for her debut novel, one more time she brings Indian English writers to the forefront all over the world. In sum, it can be said that the fictional world of

Indian English writers encompasses a whole range of themes and tend to associates with freedom struggle, partition holocaust, social evils, casticism, religion, low status of women, poverty, corruption and so on. The fresh crop of writers has adopted varied themes and style of narration and more confident approach to the fiction writing. As Atiya Singh surveys…

> "More modern themes like man's sense of alienation depicted in newer modes of narrative technique, in what has become to be termed as 'the psychological novel' also present clear contrast to the earlier modes of simple narrative techniques. … With it the Indo-Anglian literary tradition has come to acquire a new character, and wider acceptance."[6]

The genre of Indian English is a rich and varied. Chitra Banerjee Divakaruni commands a deserved mention among Expatriate Women Writers. Her contribution to this genre include: *Sister of My Heart, Arranged Marriage, Leaving Yuba City, The Mistress of Spices, Black Candle, The Unknown Errors of our Lives.*

Salman Rushdie, Amitav Ghosh, Vikram Seth, Vassanji, Bharati Mukherjee, Chitra Divakaruni, Rohinton Mistry, Shashi Tharoor, Anita Desai, Jhumpa Lahiri, Meera Syal, Amit Chaudhury, Meena Alexander, Sunetra Gupta, Gita Mehta, Suniti Namjoshi, Shani Mootoo, Anurag Mathur, Amulya Malladi, Vineeta Vijayaraghavan, Anita Rau Badami, Abraham Verghese, Peter Nazareth, Shashi Tharoor and several others are still contributing to enrich the Indian English literature. In present time, most of them have been heavily influenced by the various literary movements taking place into west and largely spreading around the world such as symbolism, surrerilism, existentialism, absurdism, confessional poetry, modernism, postmodernism and the expatriate writing. These authors use Indian phrases alongside English words and try to reflect a blend of the Indian and the other cultures.

The blend of cultures as shown by the use of language in many Indian English writers is also revealed by diaspora writers like in *The Inscrutable Americans* by Anurag Mathur, *The Namesake* by Jhumpa Lahiri, *Evening Is The Whole Day* by Preeta Samarasan and many others. These writers gave much needed oxygen to English literature with their crisp, tongue-in-cheek and realistic fictions that were read all over the world. The present condition of English literature is heartening. These new crops of English language writers are replacing the old breed and are representing India through their unique writings. Many of them have even won prestigious Booker awards and Pulitzer prizes.

VI

The quest and assertion for identity has become the most common characteristics of Indian diaspora writers. Many of the works of diapora writers reflect the meditation over the problem of search for identity. The dispossessed person's search for identity and alienation is commonplace theme in modern fiction, but for most Indian novelists in English this quest has a particular Indian immediacy. The Indian novelists' treatment of alienation, their persistence delineation of rootless characters and an awareness of his unfortunate predicament are symptomatic of their own problems.

The contemporary literature, which deals with emotional problems, clearly reflects condition of man in modern society. Getting uprooted from the native cultural traditions and values, the loss of indigenous language, the expatriate position as a mere outcast or an unaccomodated alien together with multiple affliction on the psyche, all account for the theme of 'identity atrophy' in expatriate fiction. For expatriate writers, Shyam Asnani rightly says,

> "Though the writer's individual talent should be rooted in the tradition of a particular society and culture, the real strength of the modern literary imagination lies in its evocation of the individual's predicament in terms of alienation, immigration, expatriation, exile and his quest for identity."[7]

Culturally and linguistically estranged as the individual feels about himself or herself, the whole question of his emotional, social, ethnic or cultural identity assumes mythic proportions and thus it becomes an unattainable ideal to achieve. Edward Said has discussed confusion and predicament of Indians and he approves 'the common contention' about these writers who are "neurotic, schizophrenic, ambivalent, suspended between two worlds and rooted in neither."[8] Victor Anant has analyzed the predicament of typical Indian as 'a shuffling, sleepwalking mass'. Most writers, to me, are

> "…homeless orphan… children of conflict, born in transit…smugly… and comfortably on the borderline, battening on the profits that derive from playing the role of cultural schizophrenic."[9]

Expatriate writing is multicultural and draws upon more traditions than one, and adopts a variety of approaches. Diasporic writing now focuses on culture, the differences in the cultural heritage and the ability or otherwise of rejecting, or discarding or growing with it. Because of the inherent conflict in the lives of immigrants and the constant beckoning of a personal or a historical past, the writing of expatriate is vibrant with new approaches and strategies. Expatriate writing assumes an increasingly positive approach to immigrant's multicultural reality.

VII

Among such many expatriate writes I propose to observe the works of Jhumpa Lahiri and Preeta Samarasan by comparative study of thier novels respectively *The Namesake* and *Evening is the Whole Day*. Jhumpa Lahiri won Booker Prize for her debut short story collection *Interpreter of Maladies*. Her debute novel Namesake (2003) is also sound in the theme of cultures, a confluence of Indian - American cultures. Her *The Namesake* is actually extension of various themes which she portrays in her short stories. She has beautifully captured the pain of being in between and hence nowhere. Like Lahri, Preeta Samarasan is the one such writer who narrates the experiences of being an immigrant family. She has depicted the life of the Indian origin family on the land of Malaysia. Here, the situation is altogether difference from that of *The Namesake*. *The Namesake* is a tell of first generation Indian immigrant family in America and how gradually generation gap rises among them while *Evening is the Whole* is a tell of the Indian family that has migrated to Malaysia since generations and there is not as such talk of generation gap but the uprooted condition of the Indian family in Malaysia. The Indians are not given first citizenship in Malaysia. Therefore they have altogether different problems than that of the Indian immigrant family in

America. Samarsan has depicted nitty-gritty of their lives on the after generations alien land.

In this research finds out the various issues that are pertaining to Indian English literature, Indian women writers in English, Expatriate literature, the postmodernism in literature and its effect on the writings of Lahri and Samarasan, the cultural various, the experience of being uprooted, the various presentation techniques of their literary works, the experiment that are made, the various themes that are dealt in these novels etc. by comparative study of the above *The Namesake* and *Evening is the Whole Day*.

The research work is divided into five chapters. The first chapter is *Introduction.* It opens up the subject and orients. It leads the reader through the novel as genre, the hypothesis of this research work, the Indian English literature, and the Indian diasporic tradition of writing.

The second chapter evaluates Jumpa Lahiri's *The Namesake*. The evaluation is in terms of novel as genre, plot, themes, expatriate literature, the Indian family's western encounter, their longing for their roots, narrative techniques, use of language etc. The third chapter evaluates *Evening is the Whole Day* as a novel and as a novel of diasporic tradition. It evaluates the novel as a genre, the novel as a diasporic writing, the immigration family in Malaysia, the plot construction, themes, narrative techniques, style, use of language etc. The forth chapter primarily evaluates the novels in light of each other. It differentiates the two different Indian diasporic traditions of writing. It comparatively studies the Indo-US and the Indo-Malay diasporic traditions that are Indo-West and Indo-East traditions. It compares the two different cultures of West and East and the place of Indian immigrant families in these two culturally different nations. It also studies the novel comparatively in terms of plot, themes, narrative techniques, language, influences etc. The fifth chapter summaries the whole discussion and counts the objectives that are achieved at the end of this research work.

References:

1) M. H. Abrams, *A Glossary of Literary Terms*, 7th Ed., Thomson Business International India Pvt. Ltd., New Delhi, 2006

2) Damrosch, David, "Rebirth *of a Discipline: The Global Origins of Comparative Studies*", *Comparative Critical Studies* (British Comparative Literature) 3 (1): 99–112

3) http://en.wikipedia.org/wiki/Comparative_literature

4) Walsh William, *Indian Literature in English*, Longman, 1990

5) Atiya Singh, an article *Trends in Indo-English Fiction*, from *Spectrum History of Indian Literature in English* by Sewak Singh, Charu Sheel Singh, Atlantic, 1997

6) Ibid.

7) Anthony Burges, Review of the *The Circle of the Reason, New York Times Book Review*, (6th July 1986), pg. 6

8) Atiya Singh, an article *Trends in Indo-English Fiction*, from *Spectrum History of Indian Literature in English* by Sewak Singh, Charu Sheel Singh, Atlantic , 1997

9) Asnani, Shyamal M. '*Identity Crisis of Indian Immigrants: a Study of Three Novels*', Writers of the Indian Diaspora, Ed. Jain Jasbir, New Delhi: Rawat Publication, 1998

10) Said, Edward, *The Intellectuality Between Tradition and Modernity: The Indian Scene*, The Hague, 1961

11) Victor, Anant, '*Three Faces of an Indian Alienation*', Ed. Timothy O'Keefee, McGibbon and Kee, 1960

Chapter II

The Namesake and *Evening is the Whole Day* in the Light of Each Other: A Comparative Study

Any literary work can be better understood in light of other. This is how Comparative study of literature is born, to understand one literary work in light of another. Comparative study of literary works is for understanding and seeing through the literary works of different cultures, different languages, different nations, and different ages.

The study of comparative literature is as old as single literature. Comparative Literature does not confine itself to any particular language or country nor does it create relationships with any single literature. It moves irrespective of any particular discipline. Tötösy de Zepetnek, Steven says,

> "Comparative Literature is the study of literature beyond the confines of one particular country and

> the study of the relationships between literatures on the one hand and other areas of knowledge and belief such as the arts(e.g. painting, sculpture, architecture, music) philosophy, history, the social sciences(e.g. politics, economics, sociology), the sciences, religions etc. on the other hand. In brief it is the comparison of literature with other spheres of human expressions."[1]

It is clear that comparative literature is not confined to the literature of one country. To compare one author with another, one literature with another, the literature of one period with that of another, one literary genre with the other arts is the traditional activity of the literary scholars and the critics. With the emergence of national literature the scope of such comparison cuts across the linguistic frontiers as well as national boundaries. In other words,

> " Comparative literature is an interdisciplinary field whose practitioners study literature across national borders, across time periods, across languages, across genres, across boundaries between literature and the other arts (music,

painting, dance, film, etc.), across disciplines (literature and psychology, philosophy, science, history, architecture, sociology, politics, etc.). Defined most broadly, comparative literature is the study of "literature without borders."[2]

The activities in Comparative Literature include, for example, studying literacy and social status, studying medieval epic and romance, studying the links of literature to folklore and mythology, studying colonial and postcolonial writings in different parts of the world, asking fundamental questions about definitions of literature itself. What scholars in Comparative Literature share is a desire to study literature beyond national boundaries and an interest in languages so that they can read foreign texts in their original form. Many comparatists also share the desire to integrate literary experience with other cultural phenomena such as historical change, philosophical concepts, and social movements.

Hence, the following traits of Comparative Literature can be derived. It is the study of literature not in isolation, but in comparison. It can be a comparison of two or more similar or even dissimilar forms or trends within a span of literature of the same language, for example a comparative study of the psychological conflict of Hamlet and Don Quixote. Secondly, it can be a comparison of similar and dissimilar forms and trends in literature of two or more languages, for example, a comparative study of Romantic poets with reference to Keats in English and Ramesh Parekh in Gujarati or the *Vicar of the Wakefield* in English and Raja Shekhara's *Charitra* in Telugu. It is obvious that the trends of one literature are important to establish a comparison with another literature in more than two languages.

In today's era of globalizations Comparative Study of Literature is continuously emerging and coming in the main stream literary study. It is also known as world literature as it cuts the borders of the countries and cultures. The intention of most of the scholars of Comparative Literature is to increase the understanding of other cultures, not to assert superiority over them. The same effort is done in this research work also. By comparing *The Namesake* and *Evening is the Whole* Day, from altogether geographically two different opposite directions, East and West, this research tries to bring out the qualities of these different cultures and their literary traditions.

At present time, there is an emergence of a new trend of literature that is called Diaspora Literature. Because of the growth of technology and transportation facility it has become easy to move across the borders. At present, a large number of people are migrating from one nation to another. In case of India also thousands of people have been migrating to other nations and particularly in West. They migrate, leaving behind their roots, in search of better life, sometimes for employability, better education and with many other purposes. When they are on the foreign land, in host nation, at that time they are conscious of their origin and roots. Many times it happens that they cannot fit themselves in the host culture neither they are accepted as their people. This is how they feel uprooted. They are torn in between. They are constantly in dilemma and nostalgic about their roots.

This dilemma, state of torn in between conditions and sense of nostalgia of thousands of people is voiced by many writers. This literature that identifies the crisis of self identity on foreign land and the process of self invention by being in exile is called Expatriate literature or Diasporic literature. The Diaspora traditions of writing are of two types. One is the diasporic or expatriate writing written by the writer who has been born and brought up in India and then migrated to other nation. The another type of diasporic literature is the literature written by the writers who have been born and brought up away from India and then migrated to India or their origins or forefathers are Indians.

Both of the types of writings or writers have given voice to the internal and external conditions of the people who have been away from their roots and constantly in search of their identity. Further, the writing about these experiences differs in terms of migration to different nations and cultures. People from India have migrated to almost all the nations of the world and all the Indians in different parts of the world feel their roots in India. These people have their own very different experiences of being in foreign land. Based on these experiences and crises there are further trends of diasporic writing. These trends of diasporic writing give voice to the people migrated to different nations because they have their own very unique experiences and problems like sometimes they are accepted by the host nations and cultures, sometimes they are rejected by the host nations and cultures, sometimes they cannot fit in and rejects the migrated nation or culture though they are accepted and sometimes, even though they are on the land of migrated nations since generations they are not given the rights of citizenship as the people of the respective nations, sometimes the later generations can settle down on the foreign land but the first generations feel strong tie with their origin roots and sometimes they accept their identity as fragmented and uprooted life.

At present, primarily the Indians migrate to western countries. But before years, when most of the nations were colonized by Britishers, at that time, many Indians have immigrated to the further South-East part of Asia. Many Indians travelled to Malaysia as indentured workers. Some of them returned back and some of them settled down on the land of Malaysia itself. Some people who settled down in Malaysia could make their fortune but many of them remained in poverty and hardship. Irrespective of their roots, their religions, economical background, their educational background, the Indians in Malaysia are not given the rights and citizenship equal to the Malay people. They are there, in Malaysia, since generations. Many of them have even forgotten that their forefathers had sailed to India centuries before and they are originally Indian. Even these people are considered outsiders and not treated equally and that bewilders the new generation of Indian origin in Malaysia. The people of India who migrated to Malaysia were primarily Tamil. When they migrated to Malaysia they also brought with them the Indian and particularly Tamil culture and traditions. Now there is a large community of Indians comprises 7.1% of the Malaysian population. The writers who give voice to these people's state are one type of diasporic writers. These writers can be identified as Indo-Malay Diasporic writers. Preeta Samarasan is one such Indo-Malay diasporic writer among very few. Her very first and only novel *Evening is the Whole Day* has minutely depicted the picture and place of the Indian community in Malaysia. This Indian community in Malaysia has altogether different situation than that of the Indian people in America.

America is considered to be a land of opportunity. Hence, most of the Indians migrate to America in search of better opportunities for their potential and better lifestyle. The Indians who have migrated to America have different condition than that of the people who have migrated to Malaysia. Here, people, at most, do not face racial discrimination while in Malaysia, the Indians and other communities are not accepted by the Malays and they are constantly treated as others. The Indians migrated to America again have their own different experiences and challenges, particularly keeping balance between the two cultures. The American culture differs from that of the Indian culture. Many of the Indians have to accept the new ways of American life style. Many of them fail to do so. Though they are in America, they are constantly longing for India. This state of being nowhere tears them into two. They are in constant search of their root and identity. They have to adjust to the new geographical environment that is full of cold and to the new season cycle. They have to adjust with the new Gen-X that is far more different. On one hand they want to be Indians and on the other they have to be Americans. This is the most critical situation for the most of them to balance. Many Indian literary writers have given voice to this plight of Indians in America. This tradition of writing can be called Indo-US Diasporic tradition of writing. Jhumpa Lahiri is one such writer among Bharati Mukharajee, Anita Desai, Kiran Desai, Salman Rushdie,

Kamala Markandaya, Ruth Prawer Jhabwala, Vikram Seth etc. She is a dazzling storyteller as well as novelist who won the Pulitzer Prize for fiction in 2000 for her very first short-story collection *Interpreter of Maladies*. Her debut novel *The Namesake* appeared in 2003 that again deals with the expatriate experience of the immigrant people. Lahiri considers herself an American as she stated in an interview, *"I was not born here, but I might as have been."*[3]

Lahri is quite different from the other Indian Diaspora writers writing in English. Most of the Indian fiction writers writing in English are born and brought up in India. It has almost become a fact that Indian writers writing in English do have their connection with foreign lands in more than one way. Writers like Salman Rushdie, Kamala Markandaya, Anita Desai, Ruth Prawer Jhabwala, Vikram Seth, Bharati Mukherjee etc. have migrated to U.S.A. or some other European countries if they are not born, brought up and educated there. Nevertheless what they all share is their first-hand experience with the native land which is not the case with Jhumpa Lahiri. She was born, brought up and educated in foreign lands other than India like Europe and America. Her connectivity with India and Indian people is borrowed from her grandparents, parents, books and other NRIs. She has also travelled extensively to India and has experienced the effects of colonialism as well as experiences the issues of the diaspora as it exists. She feels strong ties between her parents' homeland and the United States and England.

The case of Samarasan is also as same as Lahri's. Samarasan was born in Malaysia and raised there till her teens. She moved to USA for her higher education. She currently lives in France. Hence, it is more accurate to say that she is a Malaysian Indian Diaspora writer. Like Lahiri, She has taste of different cultures of India, Malaysia, US and now France. Her experiences are reflected in the novel also as the novel is rich with experiences of being migrated.

Both the works *The Namesake* and *Evening is the Whole Day* have autobiographical elements. As the novels are production and presentation of the writers' own experiences of being on the land of other nations, being alienated. Lahiri was born in London to Indian family and then they migrated to USA. She learnt about Indian only from their parents, books, and travelling. Like her, Samarasan was born in Malaysia to an Indian family and then she migrated to USA. After her education she migrated to France. These writers' treatment of alienation, their persistence delineation of rootless characters and an awareness of his unfortunate predicaments are symptomatic of their own problems. The characters in both the novels show the condition of the writers themselves of being in exile. Gogol, the protagonist of *The Namesake* is born in America but finds himself born between his and his parents' culture. This was the case of Lahiri also. The idea of exile runs constantly throughout Lahiri's oeuvre. In press conference at Kolkata in January of 2001, she described this absence of belonging,

> "No country is my motherland. I always find myself in exile in whichever country I travel, so that's why I was tempted to write something about those living their lives in exile"[4]

The *Evening is the Whole* is the story about an Indian family in Malaysia and set in Ipoh where Samarasan has passed her childhood. The novel also reflects the condition of Indians being in Malaysia as she herself is. In one of her interviews she said

> "I have a definite and deep attachment to Ipoh, my hometown and the location of the Big House. Although the novel is intentionally claustrophobic (we really don't leave that house much!), the atmosphere of Ipoh in the late '70s and early '80s -- its climate, its limestone hills, the rivalries between its different ethnic groups -- colours everything. As to characters: Aasha, the youngest daughter of the family, is very much like I was at age six, and for this reason I'm both immensely sympathetic towards her and very impatient with her. I thought it would be interesting to create a child just like I was, a child who watches instead of talking, who keeps secrets and distrusts everybody, and then to throw her into a completely invented situation. I never experienced anything remotely like what Aasha goes through in this novel; the whole thing is a what-if exercise, a psychological game I'm playing with my childhood self.[5]

Apart from the autobiographical elements, there are evidences of several literary influences and Intertextuality in both the novels. Lahiri quotes Dostoyevsky as saying, "We all come out of Gogol's overcoat." She also quotes Nikolai Gogol from his short story *The Overcoat* as the preface the novel. There are evidences of F. Scott Fitzgerald's *The Great Gatsby* in the narration and in scene creation.

In case of *Evening is the Whole Day*, the title itself is a line from a Tamil poem. The poem is from an anthology of Tamil classical poems *Kuruntokai* that is from Sangam literature. She also quotes the same poem in the epilogue also as discussed in third chapter. She also quotes an excerpt from the Graham Swift's 1983 novel *Waterland*. The novel *Waterland* is concerned with the nature and importance of history as the primary source of meaning in a narrative. Apart from these references, there are again and again excerpts or quotes from the Sanskrit scriptures and Hindi poems or film songs. It is an evident in *Evening is the Whole Day* that the novel is under the influence of Arundhati Roy's *The God of Small Things*. It is a novel of place and *Evening is the Whole Day* is designed in the same way.

Both the novels are bildungsromans. Bildungsroman is the German term signifying 'novel of formation'. As explained by M. H. Abrahms,

> "The subject of these novels is the development of the protagonist's mind and character in the passage from childhood through varied experiences – and often through a spiritual crisis – into maturity, and the recognition of his or her identity and role in the world."[6]

In both of the novels, the protagonists' develop through various crisis of life. *The Namesake*, the whole novel is about mental progress and self-invention of the protagonist Gogol. Gogol is imposed a name on him by his parents. He rebels against it. The novel is about this rebel and Gogol's failure to get rid of his identity. In the process of the search for his identity, he goes through various crises in relationship with his family and his intimate relations with women. Gogol achieves maturity through ups and downs of life. the novel is an account of the Gogol's inner development and at last the understanding of accepting his identity as fragmented.

Like Gogol, *Evening is the Whole* is an account of Rajshekharan. He is an Oxford returned scholar, conscious about his rights as a citizen. He wants to change the political condition of Indians in Malaysia. He is always annoyed at the fact that they are not given the equal right as the Malays though they are born in Malaysia and even their forefathers were also born in Malaysia. He faces so many ups and downs in public life as well as private life. Gradually the crises and struggle around him teach him the lessons of life and gradually grows up in a matured man. A line from the novel *The Namesake*, "Life has taught its most particular rule in very painful manner" can be applied to both of the characters as well as some other characters also.

Both the works deal with the issue of alienation, expatriate and sense of exile. *Evening is the Whole Day* deals with the problem of an Indian family being on the land of Malaysia while *The Namesake* deals with the problem of the Indian people being on the land of America. Though the themes of both the novels look alike it is different in respective context. *Evening is the Whole Day* talks about the Indian family in Malaysia and its political representation in the nation. Therefore it is very delicate issue to deal with. The Indians are in Malaysia since hundreds of years, though they do not have an equal presentation in politics, their culture, their language and everywhere else. They are hated by the Malay. The Indians are suffering from the racial discrimination. That is what the struggle of the protagonist Rajshekahar. Samarasan herself has said once in her interview that,

> "I tried to write a novel about a generation of disappointment and apathy that stemmed from the 1969 riots."[7]

Evening is the Whole Day narrates, in a very shuttle way, the generation after the 1969 racial riots. In the general elections before 1969 in Malaysia, most of the non-Malays were elected. The chapter Power Struggle shows that this fact could not be bear by the Malays. And there were massacre, racial riots in which thousands people were killed.

Though the whole novel takes place within the Big House, the canvas is broader. The Indian family is placed in the historical background of racial and class discrimination. There is always sense of fear, struggle. There is always haunting of the past. Samarasan has said that,

> "[…] Interspersed with this narrative is the story of Malaysia, and specifically of Indian immigration into Malaysia, which, despite of this family's wealth and privilege, ultimately decides their fate. Underlying the story of this servant girl and her employers is a larger story about the disillusionment and apathy of an entire generation of Malaysian Indians."[8]

The Indians in America do not have to face the racial discrimination. Their problem is the acceptance of the culture. Either they adjust to the host culture or not and this is very internal or psychological conflict. Again the problem with the Indo-American is the generation gap. First generation is rooted in their past while the next generation wants to move ahead and that is the conflict. The new generation, born in America to Indian family, is neither familiar to their root culture nor they are accepted by the culture where they are born. The loneliness and sense of exile become apparent at many places in the novel as Ashoke's loneliness and sense of exile becomes apparent from his special liking for Nikolai Gogol. Once he explains to Gogol, his son, that

> "I feel a special kinship with Gogol more than any writer... He spent most of his adult life outside his homeland. Like me."[9]

The new generation is focused in both the novels. *The Namesake* is about Gogol while *Evening is the Whole Day* is about Uma. Both are the progeny of the immigrant family. Uma in *Evening is the Whole Day* is shown a brilliant daughter of Rajshekharan. She gradually gets fed up from the hypocrisy of the elders. She is used by all the elders politically as her grandmother, Paati. Paati always takes care of her and shows that she loves her very much because she wants to take revenge against her daughter-in-law Amma by snatching Uma from her. Uma gets the same treatment by her own mother Amma also. She wants to forget her middle class roots and wants to establish herself against her mother-in-law Paati by showing herself a very good mother and getting Uma on her side. All the elders in the

Big House are in competition to each other for getting the children on their sides to prove their worth. Uma is initially tempted by it but gradually she learns the hypocrisy and politics behind it. She gets tired of the secrets and pretended love. Therefore she wants to leave the Big House and at the end she leaves it for America. She is always in struggle to understand the motives of the elders as well the behavior of the other Malays towards them. She is confused for the hatred of the Malays for non-Malays. At the end she escapes from this world of hypocrisy.

Gogol is also confused in his own way. Very first thing that confuses him is his name. The name, Gogol, was given to him very accidentally and that has nothing to do either with America or with India. It is a Russian name that has no meaning for Gogol. He always hates his name because he even cannot introduce himself in a meaningful way. Therefore he changes his name to Nikhil. But now it happens that time has passed and he cannot adjust with his new name also. He is torn in between his two names, Gogol and Nokhil. Like his name, he is also confused with his dual identity. Like his name, he rejects his origin, roots that is Indian culture but cannot even adjust to the new American culture because though the new culture does not hate him but also does not accept him as one of them. This state of being nowhere, this state of identity less, and this process of self invention lead him to struggle. At last he accepts his state as it is. He cannot run away from this ultimate situation. In that sense, both the novels are about the struggle and self invention of the new generations.

Both the novels deal with the 21st century's concepts of globalization and post-modernization. Diasporic literature itself means the literature across the borders. It moves from one culture to another culture. Both the novels are tells of the amalgamation of different cultures. Cross – culturalism, globalization are the traits of post – modern life. In 21th century, one is, on his own birth land, under the influence of other culture. In today's era technology has made it possible, and at some extent inevitable, to access the other cultures at a figure's touch. Hence, most are multi-cultured and fragmented. The same condition is talked about in these novels. *The Namesake* talks about Indo-American multi-cultured people while the *Evening is the Whole Day* tells the story of Indo-Malay multi-cultured people. Both the novels reflect the 21st century's way of life.

The beauty of the novels is in its ways of storytelling. Both the writers have adopted the flashback and flash-forward technique of storytelling. The plots of both the novels are constructed with detailed care. *Evening is the Whole Day* has very complex spiraling plot. A scene of the departure of Uma for America is torn into two. One part of the scene is the first chapter and the later part of the scene is its last chapter. In between these two parts of the scene the whole story of years is narrated by flash-bask and flash-forwarding technique. The story is told in chronological way in fifteen chapters from around 1899 to 1980. All the events that take place between these two ends of time are told in segments. Sometimes it becomes like puzzle where one has to arrange or fit the segments in a proper manner. Therefore the plot is more complex as well as interesting. Each segment of the story is designed very accurately to fit in the exact place. It puzzles as well as pleases the reader. The story opens with the Big House in Ipoh. There is struggle and hyper situation as the servant girl is dismissed for her unknown crimes and the elder daughter of the house, Uma, is leaving for Columbia. Then in second chapter, the readers are led back in time to 1899 and told the story of "the Big House beginning". Then gradually the story moves backward and forward. At the end, at last chapter, the readers again arrive at the same point of chapter one from where they have begun the journey. So it is very beautifully and compactly weaved story.

> "The plot is a delicate spiraling construction of story upon story leading you, inevitably, to a conclusion that you never thought you would reach, but which is perfect."[10]

In *The Namesake*, the arrangement of events is chronological but unlike *Evening is the Whole Day* it is sequential. The novel is divided among twelve chapters from 1968 to 2000. The novel begins with description of Ashima in her pregnancy in America. Then it leads back and tells us about the Ashima in India, her marriage, how they arrive to America, and then the story moves forward narrating the lives of Ashoke and Ashima and their children.

The first chapter establishes Ashima and Ashoke Ganguli's characters, who arrive in Boston in the late 1960s. Ashoke is a graduate student at MIT and Ashima, a homesick wife. They appear to have furiously uninfluenced by either the rising Naxalism of their land of the burgeoning Vietnam era's sensibilities of their host country. The author describes Ashima and Ashoke's previous life and the train accident in flashback. This remains Lahiri's style throughout the novel – to initiate the story from the middle and then keep on revisiting past with the help of flashbacks. Ashoke Ganguali once survived a train accident, because of Nikolai Gogol's short stories. He was lost in St. Petersburg with Akaky Akkyevich of '*The Overcoat*', when the bogies capsized. He was still clutching to the pages of the story as he lay trapped in the wreckage, and it was the site of the book that led rescuer to him that night. He was reborn on that day, and the courtesy was Gogol. This is how Ashoke moves to America and names his son Gogol. Then the whole struggle begins in America, the struggle of identity, the sense of exile, the nostalgia and the generation gap. It narrates primarily Gogol's life with his nametag that he hats. His schools, their visits to India, his relationships with two girls Ruth and Maxine, his marriage with Bengali-American family friend Moushumi, are narrated. The climax of the story is when Moushumi leaves Gogol for Dimitri. At that time Gogol is at the height of the internal conflicts. The resolution of conflict comes in story, when Ashima returns Calcutta as a widow. And Gogol realizes the origin of his true name. Gogol's self invention comes to an end with an acceptance.

The novel ends in the beginning of Gogol's new life, old identity but with acceptance as the same happens with Uma in *Evening is the Whole Day*. *Evening is the Whole Day* ends when Uma leaves for America for her new life. Both the novels are well-knit with sympathetic narration. Both the writers prolifically use the device of flashback and flash forward. There are so many places where the future is told by flash forward as the last two pages of *The Namesake* narrate Gogol's future life. There is not even a single unnecessary detail which harms the integrity of the novels.

Narrative technique refers to the way of storytelling. The voice that narrates the story is not necessarily writer's voice. Generally, an author uses narrative device to create a particular point of view from which he or she tells the story, presents the actions and thus shapes the reader's response. Through this technique the writer gives report of the external as well as internal events, but most importantly this technique expresses the angle that writer use to tell the story.

Both the novels, *The Namesake* and *Evening is the Whole Day* are narrated by the third person's omniscient narrator. There are writers in both the novels who lead the readers through. Narration is done acutely with minute details. Both the writers have used various narrative techniques like symbolism, various ironies like verbal irony, dramatic irony and irony of situation. It is evident in both the novels that the writers let life flow quietly without being intruders. All the characters are captured in their own specific condition as the characters lead lonely life in *The Namesake* is captured as below,

> "On the way to Cleveland, the journey had felt endless, but this time, staring out the plane window, seeing nothing, all too quickly he feels planes decent in his chest. Just before the landing he goes into the bathroom, wretched into the

> metal basin. He rinses his face and looks at himself in the mirror. Apart from the day's growth on his face, he looks exactly the same.[11]

Lahiri's narration describes more action of the character than the under-current of character's mind while Samarasan's characters are inspected from all the sides. She goes into each and every detail of the characters and shows their external as well as internal world. In fact, she has devoted her chapters to individual character. In each chapter there is a leading character. The story comes behind them.

Again both the writers emphasize more on the narration of the places at length. Through minute details, they create the picture of words that can be visualized while reading. In fact, Samarasan herself said that *Evening is the Whole Day* is a claustrophobiic novel. She goes into details of the scene that the reader feels as if s/he is watching the novel. One such evident from *Evening is the Whole Day* is as below,

> "It is dusk that aching, violet dusk that has come to seem the permanent state of this whole year.

> Just as Uma reaches the garden shed the streetlights come on, and clouds of moths and beetles appear from nowhere, as if they've been waiting for this moments all day. They divided themselves into equal clusters, even around the one streetlight that flickers on and off and on and off all night but refused to die."[12]

The same case is with Lahiri also, she observes the minute details and then show it to the readers as it is shown in one of the scenes,

> "It is the day before Christmas. Ashima Ganguli sits at her kitchen table making mincemeat croquettes for a party she is throwing that evening. They are one for her specialties… Alone, she manages an assembly line of preparation. First she forces warmed boiled potatoes through ricer. Carefully she shapes a bit of the potato around a spoonful of cooked ground lamb, as uniformly as the white of a hard-boiled egg encases its yolk. She dips each of the croquettes, about the size and the shape of a billiard ball into a bowl of bitten eggs, then coats

them on a plane of bread crumbs, shaking off the excess in her cupped palms."[13]

Through narration of minute details they create a word picture of the novel. The readers feel as if s/he is not reading a story but watching a story. Through this compact, integrated and lavish narration, the readers can visualize the characters also. In both of the novels, it is not difficult for the readers to create the images of the characters. In fact, the characters are shown in a way that the readers feel that they have met the characters outside the novel. One exactly can see the inner conflict and external problems of Gogol in *The Namesake* and Raju or Chellam Servant in *Evening is the Whole Day*.

In fact, the characters are more important than the story because the story cannot stand on its own without characters. To get the story well, one must get along with its characters, for it is their story. This becomes more important in the case of both the writers as their characters are not mere protagonists of the story but they also represent the different traditions.

As there is responsibility of the tradition on the shoulders of the characters, Lahiri's characters are meditative. They indulge in nostalgia and engage in intro/retrospection as throughout the novel Gogol introspects about his identity and Ashima retrospect about her past in India. Her mode of characterization is direct. She directly intervenes and informs us about the mental makeup of her characters. Her minute description of characters explains the personality and behavior of the characters. Her characters are alienated and are in struggle on the foreign land. They are displaced culturally as well as geographically. The characters are realistic and stand for the whole diasporic Indian community. To show the generation gap between the fist immigrant generation and the subsequent generation she beautifully chiseled the characters of Ashoke and Gogol.

Lahiri, prefers lifelikeness of her characters. She provides the physical description of the character, then about character's peculiarity and then slowly she would shift the narration in that character's psyche. She creates a word picture of the character that can be visualized by the reader. In *The Namesake* Ashima is the most evolved character. She is a home sickness and her nature is nostalgic. Ashoke is the ambitious and adventurous character. One train mishap led him to America. He is very fond of a Russian writer Nikolai Gogol because he passed his whole life outside in nostalgia. Gogol is the protagonist of the novel who continuously struggles for his identity and at the end accepts his identity as fragmented. Apart from these characters, there are other minor but significant characters also like Moushumi, Ruth, Maxine etc.

Samarasan has characters from all the different strata of the society. *Evening is the Day* has characters from aristocratic class as Rajshekharan, Uncle Ballroom, from middle class as Amma, and her whole family, Valli and Subru, from the very poor class as Chellam Servant and her whole family, from different professions like advocate as Raju himself, politics, shopkeeper as Raju's mistress. Keeping in mind ethnically complex situation of Malaysia, she has chosen characters from the different ethnic group like there are Indians, there are Chinese, there are Malays and there are Britishers etc. *Evening is the Whole Day* has range of characters from different age groups as Aasha a little baby, her elder brother is of around fifteen year old, Uma the elder daughter around twenty and Chellam Servant, Amma and Appa mature family members and Paati mother of all, eldest around sixty. There are also references of the people who are born by the Indian and Chinese like Raju and his mistress's children are chindians. This variety of from all the areas of life creates the whole picture of the society. Though the story takes place within the Big House, it comprises the whole picture of the Malaysian society by showing the range of characters from all the areas and this becomes strength of the this novel. In fact, much things or incidents do not happen in *Evening is the Whole Day*. It is domestic novel where the place and the characters become superior to story. The plot of the novel also depends on the characters. At many places, it seems that even the Big House is one of the many characters. It sees all the happenings around from the time of Britishers. When nobody knows anything, the Big House knows everything, it knows all the peoples' secrets, it knows the ill-treatment of Amma with Paati, it know what Raju did with her elder daughter Uma on that night but Big House is unable to say and change anything as Uncle Ballroom.

The language that is used in both the novels is unique and rarely seen. It is unique because the language is mixture of various other languages in both the novels. As it is said earlier, Jhumpa was born in London to an Indian family. At her teen age, the family migrated to USA. She represents a culture which is her origin but culturally she is more close to the country where she has been brought up. One can find the traces of the language of the country where she has passed her formative years i.e. England. Her language is fusion of English from all the three continents: Asia (India), Europe (England), and USA (Boston). There is an amalgamation of all such languages as well as presentation of cultures through language.

Like Lahiri, Samarasan has also richly used language representing different cultures. *Evening is the Whole Day* is polyglot work as it represents ethnically diverse land of Malaysia. Samarasan has beautifully handled the language and has given life to the words. She has used the language as per the demand of the characters as many of the characters use Manglish. Manglish is the English under heavy influence of Malay language. To make situation alive on pages, different characters speak the contextual language as many characters speak Tamil words again and again. The characters' background is represented by their use of language as the use of language by Amma, by Chellam, by Raju's Chinese mistress, by Raju, by Chellam's father Muniandy. There is use or references of the different language like Chinese, Tamil, Malay, Hindi, Sanskrit, Urdu and English in its different forms hence *Evening is the Whole Day* is polyglot work.

Apart from that, Samarasan herself has been dwelling in different nations. She was born in Malaysia to an Indian-Tamil family. She lived there till her teenage and the left for USA for her education. She now leaves in France. One can trace the glimpses of the influences the influences of different languages of these different nations. Primarily there is beautiful use of Manglish. The use of this typical language in *Evening is the Whole Day* reflects the land of Malaysia.

Like language, food is an identity of culture. This identity is explored in both the novels. Both the works are rich in taking note of the different items to represent the different cultures. As the land of Malaysia is multi-cultured, Samarasan has referred the Tamil, Malay,

Chinese, English food items. Like her, Lahiri also uses food to represent different cultures like Indian-Bengali and American culture as well as the fusion of cultures. Both the writers have used food as the metaphor of the cultures and fusions of the cultures in 21st century.

As the title of this chapter says, the two novels *The Namesake* are *Evening is the Whole Day* are evaluated in light of each other. Both the novels belong to the culturally and geographically different regions. Both the novels present the two different diasporic literary traditions, Indo-US and Indo-Malay diasporic literary traditions. This chapter has evaluated both the novels in terms of the literary traditions, themes, plot construction, narrative techniques, literary influences, languages and food as cultural presentation.

References:

1) Steven, Tötösy de Zepetnek,. "*Bibliography of (Text)Books in Comparative Literature.*"

2) http://en.wikipedia.org/wiki/Comparative_literature

3) Minzesheimer, Bob. "*For Pulitzer winner Lahiri, a novel approach*", USA Today, 2003-08-19.

4) www.rediff.com/news/2011/jan/11jhum.htm

5) Bradley, Winterton, *The Long Evening Wanes*, http://www.taipeitimes.com/News/main/history/2008/08/03, Aug 03, 2008

6) M. H. Abrams, *A Glossary of Literary Terms*, 7th Ed., Thomson Business International India Pvt. Ltd., New Delhi, 2006, Pg 86

7) Amardeep Singh's Interview with Preeta, appeared on internet, Tuesday, June 10, 2008

8) Review: "*Preeta Samarasan's Evening is the Whole Day*", June 10, 2008, appeared on http://sepiamutiny.com/blog/2008/06/10/review_preeta_s

9) Lahiri, Jhumpa, *The Namesake*, 2003, Harpers Collins, New India, pg: 77

10) Book Review by Nalini Iyer, International Examiner appeared on http://preetsamarasan.com

11) Lahiri, Jhumpa, *The Namesake*, 2003, Harpers Collins, New India, pg: 179

12) Samarasan Preeta, *Evening is the Whole Day*, Harper Collins Publishers – India, Noida, 2008, pg 30

13) Lahiri, Jhumpa, *The Namesake*, 2003, Harpers Collins, New India, pg: 274

Chapter III

Splitting Selves

The prime objective of this literary research was to explore the new literary works of today's era. The efforts have been made to identify the new trends of literature. In 21st century, post-modern literary works have gone under drastic changes ranging from the theme to the narrative techniques. It has been a humble effort in this literary research work to recognize the new trends, change and challenges of today's literary world.

This recognition and identification of the new literary trends, changes and challenges have been made possible by the comparative study of the two novels, *The Namesake* and *Evening is the whole Day*, by the new emerging writers. Both the writers, Jhumpa Lahiri and Preeta Samarasan represent today's young generation of the literary writers. More to it both are women writers. Hence, this comparative study of the two novels not only looks at the literary writings but also to the new generation of women writers. One thing is evident that unlike older generation of Indian English writers like Raja Rao, Mulkraj Anand, R. K. Narayan, most of the writers of today's era are multi-cultured and globalized as Lahiri and Samarasan both have lived and having very close experience of more than one culture.

The new generation of 21st century is a post-modern product of globalization that is borderless or that lives across the cultures and the writers, Jhumpa and Samarasan, are also not exception to it. This way of living in a borderless world and across the cultures has given rise to the Diaspora literature. It captures the experiences of the people who have been away from their own land. Sometimes, the writers have also been in such a situation or have undergone from the same experience. Hence, they can better understand and narrate the nuances of being on a foreign land or sometimes even in a state of exile.

Both the writers Jhumpa and Preeta are such writers who have undergone from the experiences of being in a state of exile and uprooted. Jhumpa was born in London to an Indian family and at her teen age migrated to USA. Preeta has been born in Malaysia to an Indian family and migrated to USA for higher education and now leaves in France. This touch of different cultures and the state of being away from mother culture made them to recognize their mother culture that is Indian and that is the reason behind *The Namesake* and *Evening is the Whole Day*.

Both the novels have captured the experiences of being in exile. Both the novels question the self identity by being on the other land. Both the novels are the delegates of the two different English diasporic literary traditions: Indo-US and Indo-Malay.

This research work has tried to identify, at the first level, these two diasporic traditions. Out of these two diasporic traditions, the Indo-US diasporic literary tradition has been recognized very early and explored a lot. But the Indo-Malay diapsoric literary tradition in English is never explored. So, at first, this literary work tries to name and define these traditions. As mentioned earlier that the Indo-Malay tradition is not explored before. Hence, to understand it better, it is studied in comparison to Indo-US diasporic literary tradition. This makes it easy to understand the uprooted, displaced and torn in between Indians who live on the land of America and on the land of Malaysia.

Firstly, this work explores, in first chapter, the areas like Indian English literature, Indian English Diaspora literature, women in Indian English Diaspora literature, and current trends in English literature at global level and primarily discusses Comparative literature. It introduces the Diaspora literature, the Diaspora writers and the Indo-US and Indo-Malay Diasporic traditions of literary writing.

The chapter two evaluates Jhumpa Lahiri as Indo-US Diaspora writer and primarily studies *The Namesake* as the work of Indo-US Diaspora literature. It evaluates the themes, the plot construction, the techniques for plot construction that are flashback and flash-forward, the narrative techniques that are the third person omniscient narrator, symbolism, irony. It also observes the language of the work that is the English influenced by Indian English, British English, American English and sometimes Bengali. It primarily observes that how the novel represents the different cultures and the people who are torn in between.

The third chapter is an evaluation of *Evening is the Whole Day*. It evaluates the novel as the first and the only work of Indo-Malay Diasporic English literature. Because it is the only novel of this tradition it becomes emblem of it. The third chapter also sees Samarasan as the first writer of this tradition and takes in account her as an expatriate writer. Here, the novel is evaluated in terms of the themes like migration, political power game in multi-ethnic Malaysia, search of identity, amalgamation of cultures etc., the plot construction that is spiraling and continuously moving backward and forward, the narrative techniques like third person omniscient narrator, symbolism and irony. It evaluates the polyglot language of the novel. As Malaysia is multi-cultural land, a number of languages are spoken simultaneously by different communities. Samarasan has aptly reflected this multi-cultured land by using polyglot language. Though the novel is in English, there is now and then use of various languages like Tamil, Chinese, Hindi and Sanskrit, Malay and Manglish. *Evening is the Whole Day* mirrors the land of Malaysia and the Indian immigrants on the land of Malaysia.

The fourth chapter studies both the novels comparatively. It tries to identify the difference as well as similarities between Indo-US and Indo-Malay traditions of Diaspora literature. This chapter comparatively studies both the writers, both the works, the themes, the plots, the characters, the characterization, the narration, the narrative techniques, the description, the languages, the cultural presentation, the epilogues, and the influences and inter-textuality in both the works. It also studies the limitations of both the writers and works. And the fifth chapter summarizes the previous chapters.

The objectives of this research work that were set at the beginning are to study the Indian English literature, to study the Indo-US and Indo-Malay Diasporic English literary traditions, to study the new generation of writers coming from altogether different literary traditions, to evaluate the novels comparatively and to provide insights of the current Diaspora literature. Every honest effort is made to meet these objectives. Keeping in mind the space for research, many areas might not have been touched. In future these areas of the literature may be studied and might be brought in front of the world.

BIBLIOGRAPHY:

Primary Source:

1. Lahiri, Jhumpa, *The Namesake*, 2003, Harpers Collins, New India
2. Samarasan, Preeta, *Evening is the Whole Day*, Harper Collins Publishers – India, Noida, 2008

Secondary Source:

3. Prasad, Amarnath, *New Lights on Indian Women Novelists in English*, 2004, Sarup and Sons Publication, New Delhi
4. Atma Ram, *Interviews with Indo-English Writers*, Calcutta, 1997
5. Viney Kripal, *The Thirdworld Novel of Expatriation*, 1989, Sterling Publishers, New Delhi
6. King-Kok, Cheung, *An Interethnic Companion to Asian American Literature*, 1997, Cambridge University Press
7. Ronald Taft, "*Migration Problems of Adjustment and Assimilation in Immigration*", Psychology

and Race, ed. P. Watson, Penguin Education, London, 1973

8. A. Avadesh, K. Srivastava (ed), *"Alien Voices: Perspectives on Common Wealth Literature*, Print House, Lukhnow, 1981

9. M. H. Abrams, *A Glossary of Literary Terms*, 7th Ed., Thomson Business International India Pvt. Ltd., New Delhi, 2006

10. Walsh William, *Indian Literature in English*, Longman, 1990

11. Asnani, Shyamal M. *'Identity Crisis of Indian Immigrants: a Study of Three Novels'*, Writers of the Indian Diaspora, Ed. Jain Jasbir, New Delhi: Rawat Publication, 1998

12. Said, Edward, *The Intellectuality Between Tradition and Modernity: The Indian Scene*, The Hague, 1961

13. Victor, Anant, *'Three Faces of an Indian Alienation'*, Ed. Timothy O'Keefee, McGibbon and Kee, 1960

14. Kamil Veith Zvelebil, *Companion Studies to the History of Tamil Literature*

15. Jabir Jain (Ed.), *'Writers on the Indian Diaspora'*, Rawat Publication, New Delhi, 1998

16. Iyengar, K. R. S., '*Indian Writing in English*', Sterling Publication, New Delhi, 1984
17. Naik, M. K., '*A History of Indian English Literature*', Sahitya Akademi, New Delhi, 2002
18. Pathak, R. S., '*Modern Indian Novels in English*', Creative Books, New Delhi, 1999
19. Singh and Singh, '*Spectrum History of Indian Literature in English*', Atlantic Publication, New Delhi, 1997
20. Timothy O'Keefee (Ed.), '*Alienation*', McGibbon and Kee, 1960
21. Shil Edward, '*The Intellectual Between Tradition and Modernity: The Indian Scene*', The Hague, 1961
22. Bijal Kumar Das, '*Aspects of Commonwealth Literature*', Creative Literature, New Delhi, 1995
23. Meenakshi Mukherjee, '*The Twice Born Fiction – Themes and Techniques of Indian Novel in English*', Pencraft International, Delhi
24. K. Ayyappa Panikar, '*Indian Narratology*', Indira Gandhi National Center for Arts in Association with Sterling Publishers Private Limited, New Delhi

25. Lavina Melwani, *Interpreting Exile*, in the Hindustan Times Magazine, April 23, 2000
26. Atiya Singh, an article *Trends in Indo-English Fiction*, from *Spectrum History of Indian Literature in English* by Sewak Singh, Charu Sheel Singh, Atlantic, 1997
27. Anthony Burges, Review of the *The Circle of the Reason, New York Times Book Review*, (6th July 1986)
28. Minzesheimer, Bob. "*For Pulitzer Winner Lahiri, a Novel Approach*", USA Today, 2003-08-19.
29. Patel, Vibhuti, *An Interview with Jhumpa Lahiri for News International*, 20th September, 1999, as appeared on website www.saja.com
30. Chotiner, Isaac, "*Interviews: Jhumpa Lahiri*", The Atlantic, 2008-03-18
31. Lahiri, Jhumpa. "*My Two Lives*", Newsweek, 2006-03-06
32. Garner, Dwight, "*Jhumpa Lahiri with a Bullet*", The New York Times Paper Cuts blog, 2008-04-10.
33. Aguir, Arun, *An interview with Jhumpa Lahiri* released by A Houghton Miffin Company, Boston, As appeared on www.saja.com

34. Bradley Winterton, Book Rev. "*The Long Evening Wanes*", Appeared on http://www.taipeitimes.com/News/main/history/2008/08/03, Aug 03, 2008

35. Minzesheimer, Bob. "*For Pulitzer winner Lahiri, a novel approach*", USA Today, 2003-08-1

36. Parekh Bhikhu, '*Some Reflections on the Indian Diaspora*', Journal of Contemporary Thought, Baroda, 1993

37. Kunhi Krishna, *The Twice Born Fiction: Themes and Techniques of the Indian Novel In English*', Indian Literature Sahitya Akademic's Bio-Monthly Journal, No: 217, Spe-Oct, 2003, Vol. XLVII No. 5, New Delhi

38. Suresh Mishra, '*Diaspora and Difficult Art of Dying*', from Subaltern Studies – X, Ed. Gautam Bhandra, Gyan Prakash, and Susie Thuru, Oxford Uni. Press, 2003